C000180861

Bee
/bi/ | *noun* | a stinging winged insect

Quest
/kwɛst/ | *noun*| a long and arduous search for something

Bequest
/bɪkwɛst/ | *noun* | the act of giving or leaving a gift

150

First Published 2017
Philip Butler Freelance Bespoke Website Design & Photography
http://www.philipbutler.co.uk

© Copyright Philip Butler, 2017

All images Copyright © Philip Butler, Philip Butler Freelance Bespoke Website Design & Photography, 2017 unless otherwise stated.

All rights reserved. No part of this book may be copied, displayed, extracted, reproduced, utilised, stored in a retrieval system or transmitted in any form or by any means, electronic, mechanical or otherwise including but not limited to photocopying, recording or scanning without the prior written permission of the publisher.

The rights of Philip Butler to be identified as the Author of this book has been asserted in accordance with Copyrights, Designs & Patents Act 1988.

Printed in Manchester, UK by: Manchester Printers Ltd. (Sure, I could have had it printed abroad for cheaper, but you have to support your local economy plus their address happens to be 'The hive' so who else could I use).

This Book can be ordered directly from http://www.beequest.co.uk

ISBN: 978 1 5272 1477 4

QUEST

On May 22, 2017, an atrocious terrorist attack in Manchester claimed the lives of so many beautiful people. I felt powerless to help, but desperate to do something.

Walking through the streets over the coming days, I spotted several pieces of bee-related street art which inspired me to create a book to raise money for charity. My quest to find and photograph the bees of Manchester & Salford began.

Bee Quest contains nearly 200 photographs documenting over 120 different bees throughout both cities; from bee hives on the Cathedral roof and Coats of Arms on historic buildings through to street art, tattoos and graffiti.

100% of the profits from the sale of this book will go to Manchester-based charities. Visit www.beequest.co.uk to find out which charities are being supported.

It seems only fitting to start off the Bee Quest in Manchester Town Hall with what must be the most iconic bee in the city.

Designed by the architect Alfred Waterhouse and built between 1868 - 1877 in thirteenth century Gothic style, the exterior of the Town Hall is Grade I listed. The landing on the first floor outside of the Great Hall is traditionally know as 'The Bees'. Instead of cotton flowers that can be seen on the ground floor, this mosaic, which was laid down by Venetian craftsmen, features worker bees.

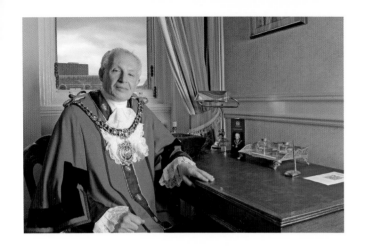

THE 120TH LORD MAYOR OF MANCHESTER, EDWARD NEWMAN, WEARING HIS CEREMONIAL ROBES THAT FEATURE GOLD BEES AROUND THE LAPEL. THE LORD MAYOR'S CHAIR AND VISITOR'S CHAIR, BOTH INCORPORATING CARVED BEES.

The portrait of Her Majesty Queen Elizabeth II was painted in 1977 to commemorate, in her Silver Jubilee year, the Centenary of the Town Hall. Below it is a sofa and opposite, an embroidery commemorating the Civic Centenary 1853-1953; both featuring the Manchester Coat of Arms (CoA) with 7 bees around a globe.

8 THE CEREMONIAL SCEPTRE (HELD BY THE LORD MAYOR'S ATTENDANT, NICK KERSHAW) WAS PRESENTED TO THE CITY IN 1895

LORD MAYOR'S SUITE: THE LGBT MANCHESTER PRIDE WORKER BEE BY CHRISTIAN TAYLOR (@CJTAYLORDART) SYMBOLISING THE HARD WORKING CITY WHICH ENCOURAGES AND INSPIRES OUR COMMUNITY TO ACCEPT, EMBRACE AND CELEBRATE LIFE.

ABOVE: MANCHESTER TOWN HALL RECEPTION ROOM: BELIEVED TO BE AS OLD AS THE BUILDING, THE BEE EMBROIDERY WAS CONSERVED IN 2004 BY THE TEXTILE CONSERVATION STUDIO AT THE PEOPLE'S HISTORY MUSEUM IN MANCHESTER. OPPOSITE: ARTS AND CRAFTS DRESSER IN THE TOWN HALL BANQUETING ROOM.

THE LORD MAYOR'S PARLOUR FIREPLACE BEARING THE MANCHESTER COAT OF ARMS AND VARIOUS FAMILY CRESTS.

TOP: THE CONFERENCE ROOM WITH A MURAL OF THE MANCHESTER COAT OF ARMS AND A FRIEZE FEATURING THE COUNTY BOROUGH OF SALFORD COAT OF ARMS. BOTTOM: CEILINGS IN THE ANTI ROOM AND IN THE TOWN HALL EXTENSION.

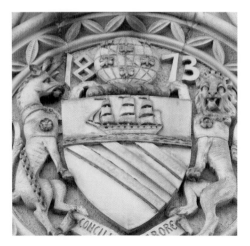

14   THE ST. PETER'S SQUARE ENTRANCE TO THE TOWN HALL WAS BUILT ONE YEAR AFTER THE ALBERT SQUARE ENTRANCE.

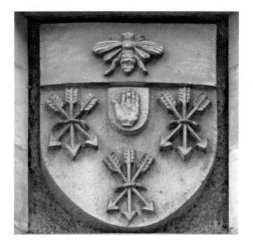

VIEW OF MANCHESTER TOWN HALL FROM ALBERT SQUARE WITH NOTABLE FAMILY CRESTS FEATURING BEES.

15

THE BEEHIVE IN THE STAINED GLASS WINDOW AND THE CARVING ABOVE THE ENTRANCE TO 53 KING STREET WAS THE ORIGINAL SYMBOL OF LLOYDS BANK AS IT REPRESENTED THRIFT AND INDUSTRY.

16

ZIZZI RESTAURANT COMMISSIONED ALICE PICKWORTH (WWW.ALICEPICKWORTH.COM) TO DESIGN & PAINT A MURAL. HER INSPIRATION WAS THE WORKER BEE.

SOME CATHEDRALS HAVE BATS IN THE BELFRY, MANCHESTER HAS BEES UNDER THE ALTAR AND ON THE CHOIR STALLS!

THE 'HOPE WINDOW' DESIGNED BY GLASS ARTIST ALAN DAVIS AND SPONSORED BY THE OGLESBY CHARITABLE TRUST. 19

20   WEEKLY MAINTENANCE BY CATHEDRAL CHAPLAIN REVD CANON ADRIAN RHODES & VOLITION VOLUNTEER TONY MAUNDER.

THE 2002 CATHEDRAL GARDENS WATER FEATURE 'SEASONS' CONSISTS OF A TOP POOL, RILL AND FINALLE POND

THE RADISSON EDWARDIAN HOTEL IS SET INSIDE ONE OF THE CITY'S MOST ICONIC BUILDINGS, THE FREE TRADE HALL.
BUILT IN 1856 ON THE SITE OF THE PETERLOO MASSACRE, WHERE ON 16 AUGUST, 1819, 17 PEOPLE WERE KILLED AND
HUNDREDS MORE INJURED WHEN CAVALRY CHARGED ON SOME 60,000 PRO-DEMOCRACY PROTESTERS.

ABOVE: TIME CAPSULES BURIED UNDER CENTRAL LIBRARY AND ST. PETER'S SQUARE, SET TO BE OPENED IN 2094 AND 2116 RESPECTIVELY. THE BEE MOSAIC WAS INTENDED TO GO INTO THE CAPSULE, BUT THE DECISION WAS MADE TO PUT IT ON DISPLAY INSTEAD. OPPOSITE: 113 DEANSGATE WITH THE SALFORD AND A FAMILY COAT OF ARMS.

ABOVE: ON 4TH JUNE 2017 METROLINK'S TRAM 3022 WAS RENAMED 'THE SPIRIT OF MANCHESTER' TO CELEBRATE THE INCREDIBLE RESPONSE OF THE LOCAL COMMUNITY FOLLOWING THE MANCHESTER ARENA ATTACK. OPPOSITE: THE JUBILEE FOUNTAIN IN ALBERT SQUARE BUILT TO COMMEMORATE QUEEN VICTORIA'S DIAMOND JUBILEE IN 1897.

THE PRINTWORKS DIRECTOR, FRED BOOTH WITH VOLITION VOLUNTEER TONY MAUNDER ON THE ROOFTOP GARDENS WHICH IS HOME TO FOUR BEEHIVES, AN ALLOTMENT, A BEETLE HOTEL AND AN INNOVATIVE HYDROPONICS GREENHOUSE.

#LiveFromTheHive project is a collaboration between the Printworks & Hard Rock Café Manchester. All the money raised from the sale of jars of limited edition honey (with labels designed by Mancsy) goes to the Booth Centre for Homeless & Forever Manchester, the community foundation for Greater Manchester.

30   A SELECTION OF TATTOO STUDIOS RAISING MONEY FOR CHARITY. STREET ART BY NATHAN SASSEN (WWW.NASARTIST.COM)

THE #MCRtattooAppeal HAS RAISED OVER £500,000 AND DEMONSTRATED AN OVERWHELMING RESPONSE FROM BOTH THE TATTOO ARTISTS WILLING TO DONATE THEIR OWN TIME & MATERIALS AND FROM THE THOUSANDS OF PEOPLE WILLING TO SHOW THEIR STRENGTH, COURAGE AND SOLIDARITY AGAINST TERRORISM BY HAVING A BEE TATTOO.

THE STAIRCASE OF THE OLD **UMIST** BUILDING ON SACKVILLE STREET BOASTS AN IMPRESSIVE STAINED GLASS WINDOW WITH BEES FEATURING ON THE MANCHESTER, COUNTY BOROUGH OF SALFORD AND THE BLACKBURN COATS OF ARMS. THE **UMIST** BUILDING IS NOW PART OF THE UNIVERSITY OF MANCHESTER WHICH ALSO HAS BEES IN ITS COAT OF ARMS.

INTEGRITY AND INDVSTRY

ET

CONCILIO LABORE

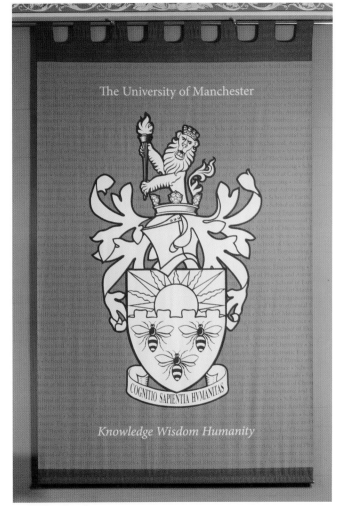

The University of Manchester

COGNITIO SAPIENTIA HVMANITAS

Knowledge Wisdom Humanity

LEFT: THE SALFORD EDUCATION OFFICES (1895), CHAPEL ST. RIGHT: UNION BANK OF MANCHESTER, CHAPEL ST.

LEFT: UNION BANK OF MANCHESTER DETAIL. RIGHT: THE SALFORD CORPORATION ELECTRICAL SHOWROOM (1928) ON CHAPEL ST. NOW THE MANCHESTER MIDI SCHOOL. CHAPEL ST. WAS THE FIRST STREET IN THE WORLD TO BE LIT BY GAS LAMP IN 1806, THE SAME TIME AS THE PHILLIPS & LEE COTTON MILL IN SALFORD INSTALLED THEIR GAS LAMPS.

THE HOTEL GOTHAM (FORMERLY MIDLAND BANK), KING STREET WAS DESIGNED IN 1928 BY EDWIN LUTYENS WHOSE WORKS INCLUDE: THE CENOTAPH - WHITEHALL, NEW DELHI & QUEEN MARY'S DOLLS' HOUSE. RUMOUR HAS IT THAT THE HOTEL GOT IT'S NAME DURING THE RENOVATIONS AS THE ARCHITECTURE RESEMBLED THAT OF THE FICTIONAL CITY.

THE LIBRARY WALK GATES, CENTRAL LIBRARY STAINED GLASS WINDOW & CENTRAL LIBRARY GLASS DOORS.

THE VILLAGE MENS FC EST. 1996 IS A GAY AND INCLUSIVE CLUB THAT WELCOMES ANYONE WHO LOVES FOOTBALL. THE MANCHESTER STINGERS WFC EST. 1999 IS A FOOTBALL CLUB WELCOMING ALL WOMEN, REGARDLESS OF AGE, ABILITY, RACE AND SEXUALITY.

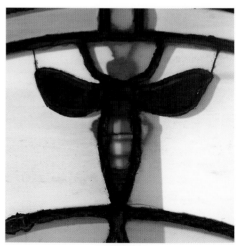

THE PRINCIPLE HOTEL (FORMER PALACE HOTEL) STANDS IN WHAT WAS ONCE THE REFUGE ASSURANCE BUILDING (1895). BUILT IN THREE PHASES, THE CLOCK TOWER WITH ITS UNIQUE BEE THEMED CLOCK FACE ALONG WITH THE MARBLE STAIRCASE FEATURING BRONZE BEES ON THE BALUSTRADES WAS ADDED BY PAUL WATERHOUSE (PHASE TWO) IN 1912.

St George's House on Peter Street was the first concrete framed building in Manchester and is Grade II listed. The present structure was built in 1911, on what was once the site of the original Natural History Museum where the 'Manchester Mummy', Hannah Beswick, was kept on display. Hannah had a fear of being buried alive and upon her death in 1758, was mummified by her doctor and kept above ground in a grandfather clock case. Her face was apparently covered by velvet cloth and in the place of the clock dial. Once a year, following the instructions in her will she was checked by her doctor for signs of life. Finally 110 years later in 1868 she was laid to rest in Harpurhey Cemetery as it was safe to assume beyond any reasonable doubt she was deceased.

THE IRWELL BRIDGE WAS BUILT IN 1877 TO CATER FOR THE INCREASING TRAFFIC BETWEEN MANCHESTER AND SALFORD.

44   Top: Manchester & Salford Bank (1869) now King Street Townhouse. Bottom: MCR barbers on Bridge St.

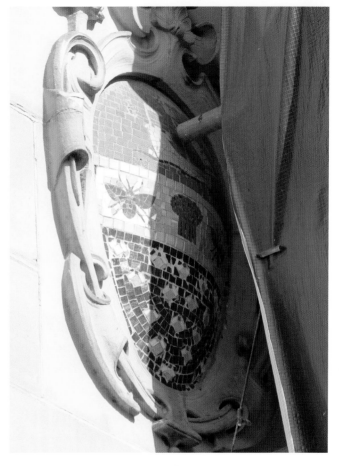

THE CORN EXCHANGE (1837, REBUILT 1903) TRADED CORN AND PRODUCE UNTIL THE LATE-40S. FROM THE MID-70S UNTIL 1996 IT WAS USED AS AN INDOOR MARKET PLACE WITH SHOPS ON THE EXTERIOR. DAMAGED DURING THE 1996 IRA BOMB ATTACK THE AREA WAS REDEVELOPED AND IS NOW A FOOD OUTLET WHICH INCLUDES COSY WITH THE MCR BEE.

PORTICO LIBRARY · 1806
THOMAS HARRISON ARCHITECT
(1744-1829)
RICHARD COBDEN   JOHN DALTON
ELIZABETH GASKELL
SIR ROBERT PEEL
THOMAS DE QUINCEY
PETER MARK ROGET WERE
READERS HERE

CONTRARY TO POPULAR BELIEF THE PORTICO LIBRARY (1806) IS NOT JUST A PUB, UPSTAIRS IS STILL A WORKING LIBRARY. FREQUENTED BY ROBERT PEEL (FOUNDER OF THE MODERN POLICE FORCE & FAMILY CREST ON THE TOWN HALL - SEE P15 BOTTOM RIGHT) AND PETER MARK ROGET WHO WAS SECRETARY AND BEGAN WRITING HIS THESAURUS HERE.

MANCHESTER ART GALLERY (1823) FEATURES BEES ON THE VICTORIAN FRIEZE IN THE PRE-RAPHAELITES GALLERY. 47

TOP: VICTORIA BATHS OPENED ITS DOORS IN 1906 BOASTING THREE POOLS AND A TURKISH BATH. IN 1993 A TRUST WAS FORMED TO SAVE THE BUILDING (WWW.VICTORIABATHS.ORG.UK). BOTTOM: THE SALFORD CORPORATION MODEL LODGING HOUSE (1893) OFFERED ACCOMMODATION FOR 285 MEN AND WAS THE FIRST OF ITS KIND IN THE COUNTRY.

PORTLAND HOUSE (c1870) ON THE CORNER OF PORTLAND AND PRINCESS BOASTS BOTH SALFORD AND MANCHESTER CoA 49

BOLLARDS, PLANTERS AND RUBBISH BINS. THE RUBBISH BIN ABOVE IS SITUATED IN SACKVILLE GARDENS WITH A BRONZE SCULPTURE OF ALAN TURING HOLDING AN APPLE IN THE BACKGROUND. AT HIS FEET THERE IS A PLAQUE THAT READS 'FATHER OF COMPUTER SCIENCE, MATHEMATICIAN, LOGICIAN, WARTIME CODEBREAKER VICTIM OF PREJUDICE'

TOP: SOUTHMILL STREET POLICE STATION (1934-37) BOTTOM: GM POLICE MUSEUM ON NEWTON ST, FOUNDED IN 1981   51

52   TOP: UNION BANK OF MANCHESTER, PICCADILLY (1911). BOTTOM: ELLIOT HOUSE, DEANSGATE (1878).

Ship Canal House (1927) on King Street. Manchester Ship Canal is a 36 mile waterway linking Manchester to the Irish Sea. Opened in 1894, it was the largest river navigation canal in the world.

Bottom Right: Detail of Lancashire & Yorkshire Bank.

LEFT: LANCASHIRE & YORKSHIRE BANK (1890) ON SPRING GARDENS. RIGHT: MANCHESTER'S FREE WIFI NETWORK

TOP: FOOT BRIDGE OVER THE BRIDGEWATER CANAL, CASTLEFIELD. BOTTOM: SALFORD BRIDGE OVER THE RIVER IRWELL

BLACK FRIAR PUB, BLACKFRIARS RD, SALFORD (1886) WITH THE BODDINGTONS' BEES ON A BARREL LOGO

58

THE SALFORD ARMS PUB ON CHAPEL ST.

ONE ANGEL SQUARE IS ONE OF THE MOST SUSTAINABLE OFFICE BUILDINGS IN EUROPE. THE THREE 'EARTH TUBES' SERVE AS AIR INTAKES AND PROVIDE LOW COST HEATING/COOLING USING THE UNDERGROUND TEMPERATURE TO HEAT/COOL THE INCOMING AIR (A TECHNIQUE THE ROMANS USED 2000 YEARS AGO).

VICTORIA SQUARE (1898) ON OLDHAM STREET WAS BUILT TO PROVIDE HOMES FOR MILL WORKERS IN ANCOATS. IT WAS ONE OF THE FIRST SINGLE-CLASS HOUSING BLOCKS TO BE DEVELOPED IN THE COUNTRY.

JOHN RYLANDS LIBRARY (1900) WAS BUILT IN THE NEO-GOTHIC STYLE INFLUENCED BY THE ARTS & CRAFTS MOVEMENT. THE LIBRARY (NOW PART OF THE UNIVERSITY OF MANCHESTER) WAS FOUNDED BY ENRIQUETA RYLANDS IN MEMORY OF HER LATE HUSBAND JOHN AND INCLUDES THE SPENCER COLLECTION AND A COPY OF THE GUTENBERG BIBLE.

CENTRAL LIBRARY'S ARCHIVES+ CONTRIBUTION TO THE READ MANCHESTER BOOKBENCH PROJECT TITLED "IF MUSIC BE THE FOOD OF LOVE... BOOKS MUST BEE...". THE PROJECT IS A JOINT VENTURE BETWEEN MANCHESTER CITY COUNCIL AND THE NATIONAL LITERACY TRUST TO PROMOTE READING AND INCREASE LITERACY LEVELS THROUGHOUT THE CITY.

GAYTHORN TUNNEL CONNECTING THE ROCHDALE CANAL TO THE BRIDGEWATER CANAL VIA THE CASTLEFIELD BASIN.

64   LEFT: COTTONOPOLIS IN THE NQ.   RIGHT: THE OAST HOUSE IN SPINNINGFIELDS. BOTH HAVE THE BEE AS THEIR EMBLEM

STAY STRONG
OUR KID ♡

BLUU BAR IN THE NORTHERN QUARTER WINDOW ART.

NEON CREATIONS (@NEONCREATIONS) RAISED ALMOST £4000 TOWARDS THE WE LOVE MANCHESTER EMERGENCY FUND BY RAFFLING OFF A NEON BEE WHICH WAS DISPLAYED IN THE WINDOW IF SOLITA IN THE NQ. RIGHT: MOTLEY STREET ART POSTER IN THE NQ (@MOTLEY_STREETART).

NOTE SKATEBOARD SHOP IN THE NQ AND VARIOUS STREET ART AROUND THE NQ.

THE M.E.N COMMISSIONED GRAFFITI ARTIST QUBEK, FOUNDER OF MURAL LIFE (@GRAFFITI_RUSS & INSTAGRAM: QUBEKMANCHESTER) TO PAINT 22 BEES ON OLDHAM ST., ONE FOR EVERY INNOCENT VICTIM OF THE TERROR ATTACK. QUBEK'S STREET ART CAN BE SEEN ALL OVER THE NQ, HE HAS A SKILL FOR PAINTING THE WORKER BEE IN MID-FLIGHT.

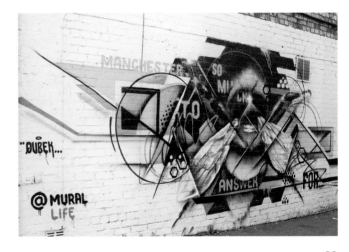

QUBEK STREET ART.

#OUTHOUSEMCR - STEVENSON SQUARE. ABOVE: PEACE & LOVE BY QUBEK. OPPOSITE LEFT: 'I ♥ MANCHESTER' BY
FREELANCE ILLUSTRATOR AND MURAL PAINTER - HAMMO (WWW.THEHAMMO.COM)

'NO FEAR HERE' BY JAY SHARPLES (INSTAGRAM: JAYSHARPLESART). 'THIS IS THE PLACE' BY TASHA WHITTLE
(@THECOLOURINGBOX WWW.THECOLOURINGBOX.CO.UK). '#WESTANDTOGETHER' BY ARTIST AMY CONEY (@AMYCONEYART)   71

THIS MURAL WAS PAINTED AT THE 2016 WELLINGTON HOUSE ART JAM (@WELLINGTONMILLMANCHESTER) BY ACCLAIMED STREET ARTISTS CBLOXX AND AYLO BETTER KNOWN AS THE NOMAD CLAN (WWW.NOMADCLAN.CO.UK / @NOMAD.CLAN)

More work by graffiti artist Qubek on Back Piccadilly Street.

THE TOP 4 FLOORS OF SUNLIGHT HOUSE (1932) ARE OCCUPIED BY THE ONLINE CAR RENTAL GIANT RENTALCARS.COM WHO COMMISSIONED GRAFFITI ARTIST KELZO (WWW.KELZO.COM) TO PAINT THE BREAKROOM ON THE 12TH FLOOR.

74

KELZO'S TRIBUTE MURAL FOR THE VICTIMS OF THE MANCHESTER BOMBING, THE PRINTWORKS, JUNE 2017.

QUBEK STREET ART AROUND THE NQ AND AT CRAZY PEDRO'S PART-TIME PIZZA PARLOUR ON BRIDGE ST. CRAZY PEDRO'S
HAVE BEEN SELLING 'UNBREAKABLE MANCHESTER' T-SHIRTS . ALL PROCEEDS GO TO FOREVER MANCHESTER

THE BRINK IS A LOCAL ALEHOUSE ON BRIDGE ST. (WWW.BRINKMCR.CO.UK) ALL THEIR BEER AND CIDER IS MADE WITHIN 25 MILES OF THE BAR. THEY COMMISSIONED QUBEK (MURAL_LIFE) TO TRANSFORM THE STAIRWELL WITH HIS UNIQUE AND DISTINCTIVE STYLE OF PAINTING BEES IN FLIGHT. OPPOSITE: MORE STREET ART BY QUBEK

Left: Peter Barber (www.peterbarber.co.uk) is a talented mural artist who was commissioned to paint the large worker bee for a client in the NQ. Right: a plaque created by @BeeMancunian, it was located on Tib St in the NQ but sadly it was removed by someone.

51/100

1/20 Valentines edition

Mancsy (www.mancsy.co.uk / @RealMancsy) has kindly given me permission to re-print his work in this book. Left: 51/100 - WW1 Centenary Poppy (thanks Fred for your generosity). Right: 1/20 - I Love MCR Valentines Edition. Mancsy makes monthly limited edition screenprints and posts them around MCR for you to find

THANKS (IN NO PARTICULAR ORDER) GO TO THE FOLLOWING FOR THEIR HELP AND COOPERATION

ALICE PICKWORTH, ARTIST (WWW.ALICEPICKWORTH.COM)
ZIZI RESTAURANT
REVD CANON ADRIAN RHODES, MANCHESTER CATHEDRAL
PAUL UPHAM, RADISSON EDWARDIAN
METROLINK (HTTP://WWW.METROLINK.CO.UK)
HOTEL GOTHAM (HTTP://WWW.HOTELGOTHAM.CO.UK)
JAMIE BROWN, THE UNIVERSITY OF MANCHESTER
BEEZ-NEEZ CAFE, 4 ASPIN LANE (HTTP://THEBEEZNEEZ.UK)
VILLAGE MENS FC
THE MANCHESTER STINGERS WFC
NICK AKA HAMMO, ARTIST (WWW.THEHAMMO.COM)
NOMAD CLAN, STREET ARTISTS (WWW.NOMADCLAN.CO.UK)
PETER BARBER, MURAL ARTIST (WWW.PETERBARBER.CO.UK)
NICOLA FERNLEY - LORD MAYOR'S OFFICE
CHRISTIAN TAYLOR, ARTIST (@CJTAYLORDART)
MOTLEY STREET ART (@MOTLEY_STREETART).
JAY SHARPLES, ARTIST (INSTAGRAM: JAYSHARPLESART)

TASHA WHITTLE, ARTIST (WWW.THECOLOURINGBOX.CO.UK)
AMY CONEY, ARTIST (@AMYCONEYART)
THE BRINK ALEHOUSE (WWW.BRINKMCR.CO.UK)
KING STREET TOWNHOUSE HOTEL & TAVERN
OAST HOUSE, SPINNINGFIELD
COTTONOPOLIS, NORTHERN QUARTER
BLUU BAR, NORTHERN QUARTER
NEON CREATIONS (@NEONCREATIONS)
REDD GLASS, WATERSTONES
NOTE SKATEBOARDS
ARCHIVES+ CENTRAL LIBRARY
CO-OP
MANCHESTERHISTORY.NET (AN INVALUABLE RESOURCE)
MANCHESTER PRINTERS LTD
(WWW.MANCHESTERPRINTERS.COM)
ANDREW NATTAN, COPYWRITER
(WWW.603COPYWRITING.CO.UK)

SPECIAL THANKS (IN NO PARTICULAR ORDER) GO TO THE FOLLOWING WHO HAVE GONE OUT OF THEIR WAY TO HELP AND SUPPORT ME WHILST CREATING BEE QUEST.

FRED BOOTH, DIRECTOR OF THE PRINTWORKS
TONY MANUDER, VOLITION VOLUNTEER
(WWW.VOLITIONCOMMUNITY.ORG)
DUNCAN McCORMICK, SALFORD LOCAL HISTORY LIBRARY
CASSIE & KAT, MANCHESTER INK
(WWW.MANCHESTERINKTATTOO.COM)
NATHAN SASSEN, ARTIST (WWW.NASARTIST.COM)
RUSSELL AKA QUEBEC (@GRAFFITI_RUSS & INSTAGRAM: QUBEKMANCHESTER)
TONY AKA KELZO (WWW.KELZO.COM)
MANCSY AKA MANCSY (WWW.MANCSY.CO.UK)

GEORGIA FROM CRAZY PEDRO'S PART-TIME PIZZA PARLOUR
EDDIE NEWMAN, THE LORD MAYOR OF MANCHESTER
NICK KERSHAW , THE LORD MAYOR'S ATTENDANT
NAMRATA CHODA, DECISION RESOURCE GROUP
MARC ROBERTS, ASSISTANT BUILDING MANAGER, THE LEXICON
THE GUYS AT SACRED ART TATTOO IN CHORLTON
AOIFE LARKIN, THE PORTICO LIBRARY
STAFF AT JOHN RYLANDS LIBRARY
BRUNO DE SOUSA
PRINCIPAL HOTEL (WWW.PRINCIPALHOTEL.COM/MANCHESTER)
PETE GARRETT - COULDNT HAVE DONE IT WITHOUT HIM